'People at Work'
IN A HOTEL

by I. & J. HAVENHAND

with illustrations by
JOHN BERRY

Publishers: Wills & Hepworth Ltd   Loughborough

First published 1972   *Printed in England*

AT WORK IN A HOTEL

Most families go away each year for a holiday and many stay at hotels. Some people have to be away from home to do their work. They may stay away from home for one night or even for weeks or months. They know that they will be well cared for in a good hotel.

There is a good hotel in almost every town. Large towns and cities have many hotels. Seaside towns have rows of hotels next to each other on the sea-front and on the roads that lead to the sea.

0 7214 0307 7

When visitors arrive at a hotel they go to the receptionist. She writes down their names and addresses and arranges for them to be taken to their rooms.

The hotel receptionist has a desk in the entrance hall of the hotel. In most hotels the receptionist is a young lady. It is important that she should be smart, well-mannered and able to talk in an easy, friendly way.

The way in which a receptionist receives guests makes them feel comfortable and at home in the hotel. They will then want to stay there again in the future.

Letters and telephone calls, from people who wish to book rooms, all go to the reception desk. The receptionist has charts which show her which rooms are empty. She knows all the rooms and tries to give people the sort of room they want. The receptionist tells the head housekeeper which rooms must be made ready for new guests each day, and which guests are leaving.

In smaller hotels there is a telephone switchboard at the reception desk. Incoming calls can be put through to guests' rooms and to all parts of the hotel. The receptionist can use a loudspeaker system to call guests if they are wanted. In large hotels there is a separate telephone exchange and operator.

The keys to all the rooms are kept at the hall porter's desk. This is in the entrance lounge. The keys have the room numbers on them. They hang on hooks on a key-board that also has numbers on it. The keys are handed to the hall porter by guests as they go out, and collected from him when they come in.

The head hall porter is in charge of other uniformed staff such as lift boys, luggage porters, doormen and night porters. A hall porter is always ready to give any inform-ation which a guest may need.

The head housekeeper looks after all the bedrooms in a hotel and sees that they are kept clean and tidy. She has a staff of under-housekeepers, room-maids, corridor-maids and linen-maids to help her.

Every day the room-maids make the beds and clean the rooms. They change the bed-linen when this is needed and put out clean towels. They try to do their work when guests are not in the rooms.

The corridor-maids clean the bathrooms and toilets and sweep the corridors. They also clean some of the lounges.

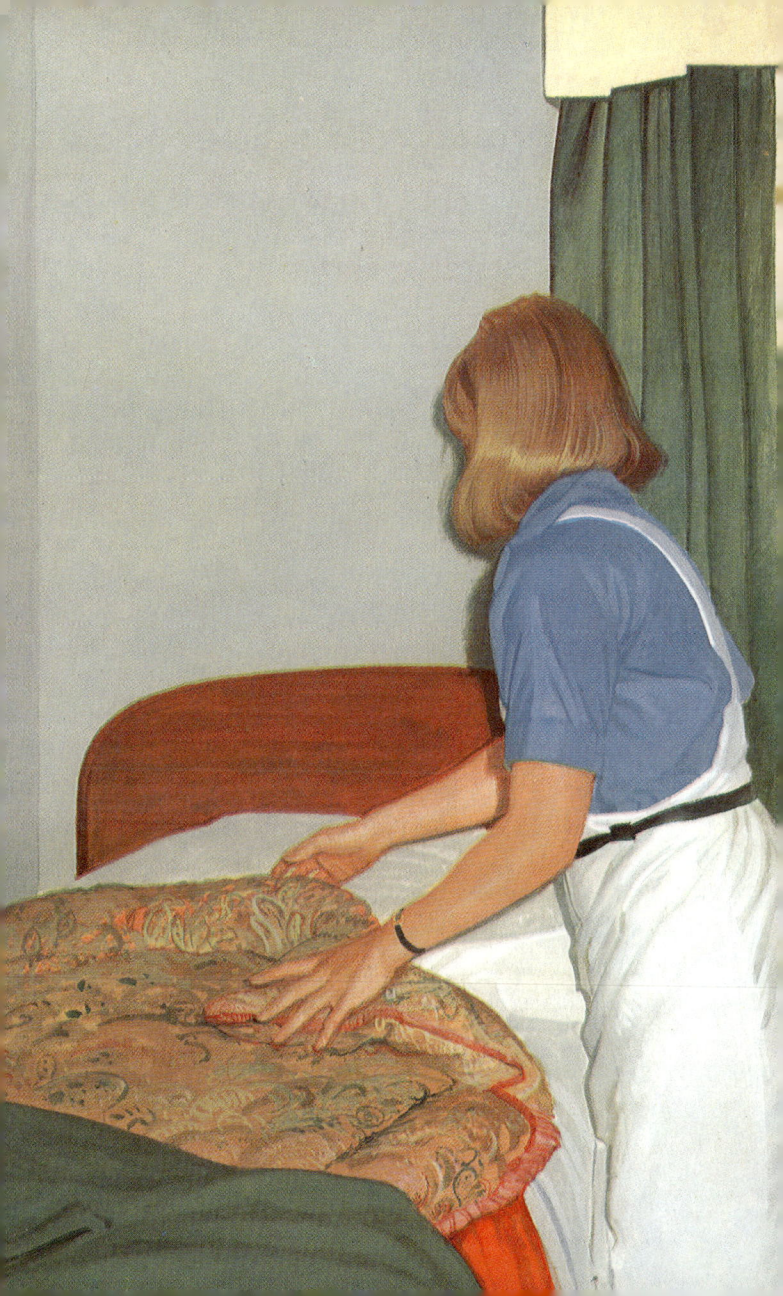

Linen-maids collect sheets, pillow cases, towels, tea-towels, table cloths and table napkins and send them to the laundry. When these articles come from the laundry, they are checked and stored in the linen room.

In hotels there is always a lot of linen to be looked after. Any linen that is torn is mended by seamstresses.

Some hotels have a valeting service. Guests can hand in, to the housekeeping staff, shirts, dresses and suits to be cleaned or pressed.

Guests are looked after in the dining-room by a man called the *maître d'hôtel*. As well as guests who are staying in the hotel, many other people visit hotels for meals.

Quite often hotel dining-rooms are booked by people for business luncheons and dinners, parties for special occasions, and for wedding receptions. The maître d'hôtel arranges everything to please the people who need the room. He will even arrange such details as the sort of wedding cake required.

The maître d'hôtel is in charge of all the dining-room staff. He arranges for waiters to take food into lounges and bedrooms if guests ask for it.

The maître d'hôtel stands at the door of the dining-room. He greets people as they arrive and hands them over to the care of a head waiter.

In very large hotels there may be more than one head waiter. Each one is in charge of a part of the dining-room.

The head waiter shows the guests to a table. He sees that they are seated and gives them the menu. The menu is a list of the many kinds of food being served. A waiter then brings guests the food they have chosen from the menu.

The different kinds of food on a menu often have French names. Waiters know the food and help guests to choose from the menu.

When waiters serve food they use a spoon and a fork with one hand. They need a lot of practice before they can do this well.

Before waiting at tables, waiters train as assistants and are called commis waiters. They carry food from the serving counter to the sideboard but do not serve guests. Commis waiters carry away used dishes and prepare the tables for each meal.

Before they start their meal, some people like to have a drink of their choice in the cocktail bar. This is prepared for them by the barman.

A wine waiter takes guests any drinks they want with their meals. The wine waiter must know all about wines, how to look after them and how to serve them.

When guests have ordered food, the order is passed over the serving counter. Another man, not a waiter, tells the chefs (cooks) what food to prepare. This man is often the kitchen clerk.

The kitchen clerk sees that there is plenty of food in the kitchen to be cooked. He also helps the chef and maître d'hôtel to fix the prices guests will have to pay for meals.

In hotel kitchens, French names are given to the food and the people who cook it. The cooks are called *chefs* and are always men. You can see one at work in the picture.

The head cook, who is in charge of the kitchen, is called the *chef de cuisine* (the French word for cooking—pronounced 'quee-zeen'). He knows how to prepare all the food that leaves his kitchen. Breakfasts, lunches and dinners all have to be prepared by his chefs. As well as being an expert cook, the chef de cuisine must be able to arrange the work of a very large kitchen staff.

The work in a large hotel kitchen is divided into sections. Each section has a chef in charge of it.

For example, there is a chef in charge of the part of the kitchen where food is made ready for the other chefs to cook. Here the meat, fish and poultry are cut up ready for cooking.

Other men cut up cooked meats to make cold meals.

In large hotels and restaurants, each part of a meal is cooked by a different chef. One chef makes all the sauces. Another chef cooks meat, another cooks fish, and others cook vegetables and soups or make cakes, pastries and sweet dishes.

The chefs have many helpers. Boys who are training to be chefs learn by watching and helping.

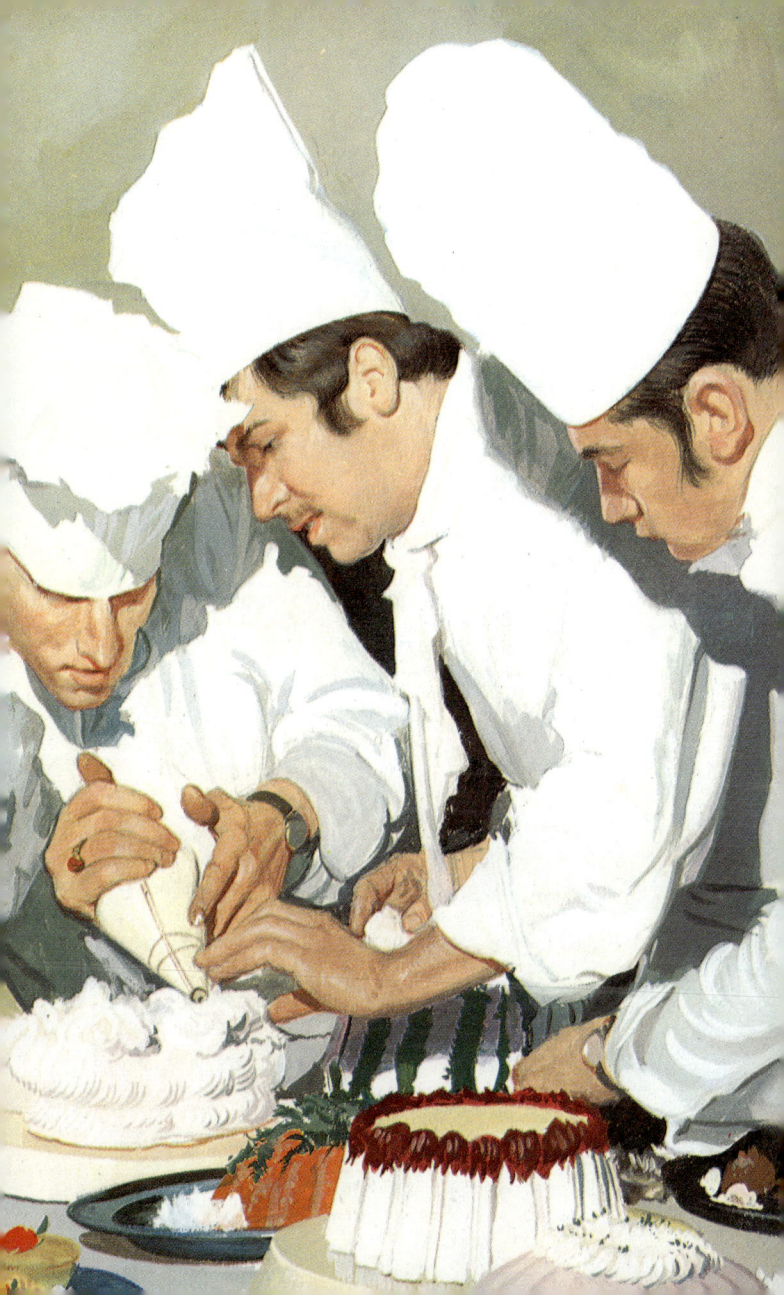

The chefs and the men who help them only cook food. They do not prepare vegetables for cooking or wash pans and kitchen tools. The chefs keep their workbenches tidy and porters carry away the things to be washed.

In a hotel there are hundreds of cups, saucers, plates and dishes to be washed. These are usually washed in dishwashing machines.

One part of the kitchen is called the still-room. Quite often girls work there making tea, coffee and hot drinks. Toast, cereals and sandwiches are also prepared in the still-room.

Guests who are staying in a hotel do not have to pay cash after each meal. When taking an order for a meal, the waiter asks a guest to tell him his or her room number. During each meal the waiter then makes notes of the cost of each part of a guest's meal. These notes are given to the head waiter who takes them to the cashier's office.

Girls in the cashier's office keep a list of all the meals, cups of tea and other services that a guest has had. The cost of all these is then listed against the room number and name of the guest. The girls use special machines for this work.

Most hotels ask visitors not to leave valuable things in their rooms. These may be left with the cashier and can be asked for when they are needed. Money can be left too, and visitors can ask for some during their stay. The valuables and money are kept locked-up in the hotel safe.

The cashier's office is usually next to the reception desk near the front entrance of the hotel. When guests leave they ask the cashier for the bill. Everything is quickly added up by a machine, and the guest pays the bill.

Most of the large hotels have 'staff quarters'. This is a part where the various hotel workers can live.

When there are no staff quarters the staff may have to live in a hostel and travel to and from the hotel.

Very large hotels have detectives on the staff. They look like guests as they walk around the corridors and sit in the lounges. Their job is to see that no one steals anything from the hotel or from the guests.

At night when guests are in bed, watchmen guard the inside of the hotel to make sure that everything is safe.

The reception halls, lounges, dining-rooms and sometimes the corridors of hotels are made more attractive by displays of flowers and potted plants.

Many different flowers and leaves are cleverly arranged to give colourful and pleasing effects. They have to be watered regularly and changed when necessary. This is sometimes done by someone in the hotel. However, large hotels often arrange for an outside flower shop to do this work for them.

In a large hotel there are many people whom the guests rarely see at work.

The floors of reception halls, dining-rooms, lounges and ballrooms have to be cleaned or polished by hotel staff. In large hotels this work is done at night when it will not interfere with the comfort of the guests. Machines are used for much of this work. These are very quiet so that sleeping guests will not be disturbed.

Engineers look after the boilers, hot water supply and plumbing, and electricians make sure that everything electrical is working properly.

In all hotels there is one man who is in charge of everything. This is the manager. Very often he lives in the hotel with his family. If he does not live in the hotel, an under-manager looks after the hotel when he is not there.

The manager usually wears a black coat, striped trousers and a dark tie in the daytime. In the evening he wears evening dress of dark trousers, black jacket and bow tie. His office is near the entrance lounge and from there he supervises the running of the hotel and the comfort of the guests.

The manager of a hotel must be a pleasant person who is able to get on well with other people. He has to be able to keep his staff and guests happy. The manager does not choose all the people who work in the hotel. He chooses only those people who are in charge of different parts of it.

The manager talks about the running of the hotel with the chief members of his staff. They discuss the prices that guests will pay for rooms and meals. The manager is always around to make sure that the hotel runs smoothly, and to deal with any serious complaints.

At holiday resorts, the managers and staff of hotels do all they can to make sure that guests have happy holidays.

Some hotels have swimming pools. Expert swimmers are on the hotel staff and are always near the pool to look after the people using it. They may also give swimming lessons to guests who want them.

In the evenings, guests may dance in the hotel ballrooms. Fancy-dress competitions are held there and sometimes concerts are given. These are organised by the manager and his staff.

Young people who want to work in hotels may do special training when they leave school.

Boys and girls can start training when they are fifteen years old and the training lasts from one to four years. They choose the kind of work they wish to do and then learn how to do it well.

Sometimes the training is done at a technical college, sometimes in a hotel, and sometimes in both. In the picture you can see a hotel chef demonstrating to student chefs.

Years ago, the most important hotels were near railway stations. Today, many people travel by car and new kinds of hotels, called motels, are popular. In these, people can make their own tea and coffee or light meals if they wish, or they can have all meals in a dining-room. Cars can easily be parked at motels, as they are usually built outside a town where there is plenty of space.

More and more large hotels are being built near airports for the use of people flying from one country to another.

Series 606B